CIRCLES
of
Beauty

CIRCLES

of

Beauty

A Portrait of Beauty, Self-Image, and Vision

GLENDA K. ROSE FREEMAN

CIRCLES OF BEAUTY
A PORTRAIT OF BEAUTY, SELF-IMAGE, AND VISION

New International Version (NIV)
Holy Bible, New International Version®, NIV® Copyright ©1973, 1978, 1984, 2011 by Biblica, Inc.® Used by permission. All rights reserved worldwide.

New King James Version (NKJV)
Scripture taken from the New King James Version®. Copyright © 1982 by Thomas Nelson. Used by permission. All rights reserved.

English Standard Version (ESV)
The Holy Bible, English Standard Version. ESV® Text Edition: 2016. Copyright © 2001 by Crossway Bibles, a publishing ministry of Good News Publishers.

iUniverse books may be ordered through booksellers or by contacting:

iUniverse
1663 Liberty Drive
Bloomington, IN 47403
www.iuniverse.com
1-800-Authors (1-800-288-4677)

ISBN: 978-1-5320-7856-9 (sc)
ISBN: 978-1-5320-7855-2 (e)

Library of Congress Control Number: 2019910299

Print information available on the last page.

iUniverse rev. date: 08/09/2019

Little girls with vision grow up to
become women with vision.
—author unknown

A circle represents totality, wholeness, being complete,
original perfection, the self, timelessness, and
movement. In the Circle of Beauty, we live and move
and have all his being. We are one with God.
—Glenda K. Rose Freeman

HELLO

Beauty

Hello,
Beauty

CONTENTS

DEDICATION

This book is dedicated to all the little girls who desire to be beautiful. I hope you will take steps to find your inner beauty first. I pray that at an early age you will be made aware of the treasure that resides inside you. Your beauty is not contingent on outward appearance only; your spirit, soul, mind, and heart must be cared for throughout life's journey. Beauty appears in unexplainable ways, and you will never fully understand it. However, you will comprehend some stages, so use them to enlighten others. Trust Mother Nature, who is part of your physical process, for she will not disappoint you, and ultimately, she will help you blossom into a beautiful woman. This book will be a compass to help enhance your character as you become the best you can be.

Many women grow up thinking their hair, complexions, and body types determine how beautiful they are, only to find that they've missed the mark. They condemn themselves for not looking like someone else or for failing to achieve a superficial definition of beauty determined by society. I devote this book to you and all those who have crossed my path. It is not too late to discover your hidden attributes and to refine, cultivate, and nurture your character. The definition of true beauty is …

Begat Eternal Attributes: Understanding Truth about Yourself

ACKNOWLEDGMENTS

I would like to acknowledge all the young girls and Perfect Pearls Mentorship Inc. You are in the design room of life, and what you imagine and create will play out in your life. The powers to create is your God-given right. You can create on demand if you use your imagination in a big way and paint your Circle of Beauty colorfully. You have affected my life in ways you will never know, so thank you for being part of my dream—and now my reality.

To my granddaughters—Destiny Maya, Dayana Christine, Dream Alana, Evony Nicole, and Genesis. As I watch you blossom, I am amazed at how history repeats itself. Each of you reflects some aspect of me. I pray I can help mentor you for your position and status in life. With love, hugs, and kisses, from Mom Mom Kai.

To my mother. Your memory is a driving force in my life. You were always a queen, and your queenship continues. Many young girls will be groomed in the "celestial courts of your memory, skill, talent, and creativity." I pray that we will continue with the things you started in excellence and love. I know that you and our ancestors are cheering us on in the celestial comics. Thank you for being my mother, mentor, and friend.

Finally, to my best friend forever, the Holy Spirit. May our relationship continue to grow forever more.

Bestie,
Glenda K. Rose Freeman

BEAUTY

Begat Eternal Attributes:
Understanding Truth about Yourself

BEGAT

Begat means to procreate as the father in your mind, to become what you were created to be. If you are unsure what you should be, just know you are wired with the answers. However, God allows us to journey to the place of discovery and adventure, so let's begin. God makes sure we all have an opportunity to choose, create, begat, and become. Our journeys will differ from season to season and their time spans will vary, but rest assured that you will experience both winter and summer. Don't despair when those chilling moments creep up on you, for you will also have seasons of refreshment and renewal. Remember you have what it takes to manifest your reality, everything is working for your good, and in due season everything will make sense. Even when it doesn't feel or look like it's working favorably, believe in what looks impossible. You will find that difficult experiences are the ultimate educators. All journeys are necessary because they qualify us to help future generations pursue similar goals and ambitions with fewer pitfalls.

It would be perfect if we prepared for the journey while in our mothers' wombs. Is that at all possible? For sure, and how so? Let's go back to the Bible. Do you remember when Elizabeth, John the Baptist's mother, and Mary, Jesus's mother, met up with each other? You know, like a girls' getaway weekend? At the sound of Mary's greeting, Elizabeth's child leaped within her, and Elizabeth was filled with the Holy Spirit (Luke 1: 41 NIV). John, the unborn child, bore witness that Mary was carrying the Messiah. (His assignment appeared before him while he was yet in his mother's womb. John was a forerunner who prepared the way for Jesus, the Son of God.) Scripture tells us that Elizabeth gave a glad cry and exclaimed to Mary, "God has blessed you among all women, and your

1

child is blessed" (Luke 1:43 NIV). Wow, that one conversation was filled with such divine insight. Elizabeth asked, "Why am I so honored, that the mother of my Lord would visit me?" She saw who Mary really was and recognized her unborn child. The Holy Spirit was at work, revealing to both women the roles they would play in each other's lives. Elizabeth wasn't a bit jealous; in fact, she was honored.

How was your last conversation with your girlfriends? Were you blessing or cursing? Were you jealous with contempt, or did you cause someone's baby to leap? We all have opportunities to speak life's blessings to women and their children. Imagine that for three months, every woman made a conscious decision to see only the good in others, with no faultfinding, gossiping, jealousy, or competition—just blessing one another with kind words and deeds. The atmosphere shifts intensely when we use positive communication, which causes us to gravitate toward one another in a positive manner. *Gravity* is defined by the dictionary at merriam-webster.com as dignity of bearing, importance, or seriousness, which can positively affect relationships. Newton's law of universal gravitation describes gravity as a force that causes any two bodies to be attracted to each other.

The communication of sound is a natural phenomenon as our words actively create our presence in the world. We are either bound or free, based on the conversations we have or listen to. Every Mary needs an Elizabeth and every Elizabeth needs a Mary to assure that their galaxies are positively influenced by each other. I am convinced that both soon-to-be mothers understood the importance of being around the right people and engaging in positive conversation. In the Circle of Beauty, everyone must connect with a Mary or an Elizabeth.

Welcome to the world of begat, the beginning of your journey toward becoming the image of God.

Beauty begets beauty.

ETERNAL

Beauty never fades, for it is eternal. According to Webster's, *eternal* means "lasting or existing forever without ending or beginning." God and Spirit are described as being always the same without beginning or ending. As we become aware of the inner and outer workings of beauty, we realize that our external beauty has an internal supernatural component that is without beginning or ending. If we depended on the eternal, we would age more slowly and have less need for surgery, although I am not opposed to safe surgical enhancement.

Have you noticed that after someone dreams about a loved one who has died, they often mention how beautiful the person looked? Beauty is an eternal attribute that persists throughout life. When we cultivate our spiritual lives, we begin to experience more of God and his eternal beauty from new angles and at various stages from birth to death. Dying to ourselves only to find ourselves is eternal rebirth. We lose our lives only to find them, we die and then live all over again, and we come back resurrected with growth in some aspect of our lives. Through life we are beautifully re-creating, rejuvenating from season to season, from age to ageless. Every wrinkle, frown, and smile tell a story.

When I was a child, my mother told me that a mole is a beauty mark. Since then, I've transformed every pimple into a mole by using a good eyebrow pencil to color it black. (It was a sensational idea.) I've had my beauty marks, and the pencil has served as a Clearasil product. I've never seen a pimple the same way, and I've been able to have beauty marks right where I want them. I just wonder why no one has ever asked what happened to my mole.

As I have become spiritually mature, I feel more beautiful now than ever. I realize that life evolves, and I am a universal spirit, a kingdom representative. The secret to eternal youth and beauty is in his presence, in communion and relationship with the one who has eternal life in his hands. We are the high-quality creation of his glory. In the Circle of Beauty, our beauty has no beginning, endlessly transforming (just like my pimple) as we get better with time. We should keep our physical bodies, minds, and emotions strengthened by doing what is reasonable and necessary to maintain wellness. However, let's not forget to bless our bodies and thank our creator for eternal life, as we represent his character on earth. What does God look like to you? I believe that he is beautiful and I am the outer semblance of his eternal beauty and love.

Your greatness awakening comes when you are
aware of your infinite nature.

ATTRIBUTES

God gives us all beautiful qualities, for he is the world's greatest designer. He designed beauty in all shapes and sizes and attached various attributes to it. I am sure he had a lot of fun in the human design room as he created beauty. You and I were able to choose which form we wanted for ourselves. God gave us the inward expression of the fruit of his Spirit, but we must cultivate it until it brings forth good character and personality. What attributes do you possess?

I have a friend whose eyes sparkle whenever she helps someone, and I can literally see and feel the joy that radiates from within her. I have another acquaintance whose eyes glitter and sparkle when she is teaching, and from what I've surmised, the fruit of the spirit ripens within her. Love and service light us up, build our character, and nourish our inner persons. Beauty is a positive attribute, yet it is downgraded to appearance—a big butt, breast, and hair. There is nothing wrong with beauty enhancement; it's when we depend solely on exterior appearances that our inner qualities fall short, and then our interior castles will be noticeably void of personal treasure. One day our bodies will shift and our facial features will change, but our inner qualities will remain.

When you are young with great features, it's hard to see past good looks that easily go unnoticed by others, but there is much more in you to behold. Even if you feel you don't have good external features, you really do. You must recognize all of you, the totality of womanhood, because what you offer to enhance and beautify the earth—your essence of womanhood—enlarges the Circle of Beauty.

I have been fortunate to coach and minister to many girls and young women, and I have a habit of staring at folks and looking at the core of their being. It is not often that the Holy Spirit allows me to see that way, but occasionally I see the soul of woman. I saw that the soul of one woman was completely depleted and empty, and I knew that I was there to help her see herself differently. I have a relative who was somewhat of a tomboy. One morning I was just staring at her and I saw her true essence. In my vision, she was dressed elegantly, and the designer in her became apparent. Go figure! I saw her inner potential despite her outward appearance.

We must think and become more than superficial replicas of public opinion and social media divas. God gave us fruit, which contains seeds and develops from the female part of the plant. We are the fruit for the entire nation, the birth canal for the world. We can discover many fruitful attributes that make us charming, ladylike, polite, intelligent, alluring, helpful, and resourceful. It does take time, self-exploration, patience, and desire to achieve our highest good. But don't worry, because we can make it happen. It's already in us. Perhaps it's not yet ripe but just needs to be watered! We often see women selling themselves short for the sake of fame, money, and notoriety. But at the end of the day, we must be able to look at ourselves in the mirror and love who we are. Let's not forget our reason for being and the purpose for beauty, and use it wisely.

You are a gift—not an object to be misused and abused. You were created to bring forth beauty in diverse ways that will enhance your world with images of character, individualism, and a positive disposition. No one can bring forth beauty like a woman, for she is the unique design of feminine presence, created by God to show his craftsmanship to the world. I admire diversity and differences, for various attributes formulate beauty around the world.

After the knowledge of, and obedience to, the will of God, the next aim must be to know something of His attributes of wisdom, power, and goodness as evidenced by His handiwork.
—James Prescott Joule

I stopped explaining myself when I realized people
only understand from their level of perception.
—author unknown

UNDERSTANDING

Understanding who you are is not easy when you don't know your purpose for existing. If I was born to be a queen but did not know my purpose in life, my upbringing, training, and trials might not make sense to me. When our daughters are young, we must pay attention to the things to which they are drawn and guide them down the runways of life that lead to their purpose. To my young lady friends, I say don't be afraid to discuss your dreams with your parents or mentors. "Where there is no guidance a people fall; there is safety in having many advisers" (Proverbs 11:14 ESV). Talk to people you can trust.

If your child adores animals, what animals is she drawn to—or does she love all animals? If she's always bringing home wounded cats or birds, maybe she'll become a veterinarian. Nurture her passion by allowing her to have experiences in the areas she shows interest in, as well as introducing her to other possibilities. Do not dismiss her choices and experiences as unimportant but give her opportunities to pursue them whenever possible. Daughters may frequently change their minds, but that's good for them, even though parents might be disappointed when a daughter no longer wants to be a prestigious lawyer. Ultimately it is up to parents and mentors to help young people shape their world through vision, character, and positive reinforcement that builds a healthy self-image.

When we have understanding, we make better decisions and choices that have rewarding outcomes. Understanding builds self-confidence and wisdom. As you understand your purpose, you begin to recognize that no one can do it like you can. It is your personal assignment, designed and created just for you. Understanding what God made us to be is the number one question most of us ask and long for. Who am I, and what am I going to grow up to be? Some of us are still deciding at a ripe old age, but it's never too late. I have seen many carbon copies of women who mimic one another. It's easier to steal someone else's personalities through observation than to develop our own. Unfortunately, many adult women are still looking for a glass slipper. On the other hand, some people are blessed to comprehend who they are at a young age. We call them the discoverers, the forerunners, as though they came to earth with understanding. We are all important and have assignments to fulfill; we just must figure it out.

Discoverers are brave volunteers who say, "Send me, Lord. I'll go and create the road maps for others." Dorothy in *The Wizard of Oz* was a forerunner. She met others along the way, but she had to master the challenges so that others could arrive. In *Alice's Adventures in Wonderland*, Alice lacked understanding and had issues with her appearance that hindered her progress. In the movie, Alice's mentor spoke these profound words: "I can't help you, Alice, if you don't know who you are." Alice had to quickly figure it out, and her huge size complemented her huge assignment. Today many of us are like Alice. We don't like our size, looks, hair, and so on, and we lack understanding that our packaging is part of our assignment.

When you pray and ask for understanding, don't be shocked when it is revealed. It will always be more than you expected, filled with challenges but never too much for you to handle. The only way to master your life is to understand the reason for it. Above all, seek understanding, which is among the most significant of abilities. You can have wisdom and knowledge, but without understanding, that equates to education with no application. Know and forgive yourself, appreciate who you are, be yourself—and above all, understand who you are and what you were created for. You are most valuable to God in helping to complete his vision for humankind.

Understanding is the bridge to self-confidence.

TRUTH

How many times have you lied to yourself or ignored the greatness that lies within you? How many people have lied and told you untruths about yourself that you believed? How many fears and doubts do you still need to overcome? All these things I previously mentioned are enemies to the human soul, and they will leave you in a state of self-conflict and accusation. Truth is a light bearer, and it will always shed light in the darkest situation. Truth opposes anything false, fake, or misleading. It is the liberator that frees the soul into a harmonious state that produces insight into realities and possibilities. Truth is an unbeatable revealer that outshines deception, no matter how long it takes. When we embrace our natural feelings and unmask the dark secrets that haunt us, truth will be the guiding light that leads to salvation and frees our soul.

Years ago, a chemical was spilled on my face and discolored my skin. As time went on, it darkened but left a scar. Every time I looked at it, I called it ugly, but God told me to call it a beauty mark. God is the spirit of truth, and he renamed my ugly into something beautiful. He would not allow the enemy of my own soul to lie to me. He saw what could be—the self-sabotage, fear, and host of lies that would shipwreck my life. I had many issues. Just like the woman with the issue of blood, I bled for many years because of rejection, deception, and fear. But when people in my life caused hurtful moments and situations, God always reassured me of the truth and delivered me from all my fears.

As time passes, you too will heal, although how long that takes will depend on the situation and how quickly you can cover it with the pure, unadulterated love of God. There will always be someone willing to lie or gossip about you, but when you walk in truth, you will end up praying for them. Naysayers are there to strengthen you for your purpose. We are who God says we are—beautifully and wonderfully made, with nothing missing or broken. The creator will never lie to his own creation. When he looks at us, he sees the fullness of who we are, and he sees us as he is.

God saw the widow woman's pitiful offering of a penny and called it a monumental moment (Luke 21:1–4 NIV). Leah was unloved, and he made her fruitful over world beauty; she birthed several famous sons (Genesis 35:23 NIV). He caused a dead girl to live and called her Talitha Koum, and she awakened to herself (Mark 5:41 NIV). He saved a widow woman and her son on the brink of death and supplied them with everything they needed (1 Kings 17:7–16 NIV). He predestined an orphan girl to live in a palace and marry a king to save a nation (Esther 1:1–2:18 NIV).

The Spirit of Truth did amazing things for women in the Bible, and today he is still at work in each one of us. He wants us to experience his truth and be transformed into something greater and beautiful. Truth can live only in the light, so there cannot be corners of darkness anywhere in your life (John 14:30 NIV). We must shun negatives that overshadow truth. Truth is the light. In the Circle of Beauty, we are overshadowed by the Holy Spirit, just like Mary was. We are seeds of love and beauty planted to bring forth daughters of light. Let your truth shine!

Fly forward
and
do not
look back

Talitha Koum

Woman, Arise

He who knows others is wise: He who
knows himself is enlightened.
—Lao Tzu

YOURSELF

Learning to love and care for yourself is an important ceremony for all women. Life is to be celebrated, privately and publicly, as often as possible. I believe that women need to consistently celebrate themselves and other women. When I come across haters, I think to myself that they have not been celebrated enough. Celebration produces ceremonies of respect, performance, commemoration, honor, and remembrance. We need to celebrate our accomplishments with humility and enjoy each moment with passion.

When I was in high school, I would try on clothes the night before celebrations and wear my selections with confidence. I applied makeup, smiled in the mirror, and examined my body. I decided what I wanted to change and then made the changes, whether it was losing a couple of pounds or exercising. I began to understand things about myself through spending time with myself. I learned at an early age to like myself and enjoy my own company, and seldom was I bored. When I was seventeen years old, I learned to love jazz and began collecting contemporary jazz albums. By the age of eighteen, I was a DJ with a slot on the radio playing jazz. A neighbor heard me playing music, took me to the radio station, and showed me how to use the equipment. I produced and mixed three jazz CDs and continued to listen to jazz daily.

When I graduated, my mother gave me a dark green journal with a gold lock and key. It wasn't the gift that I expected or desired, but it unlocked my creative writing skills. Some things you learn through experimenting, they will make sense as time passes, every event is a treasure, and the value appears later in life. I learned more about myself through journaling, writing, and music. Years later, I read my journal and enjoyed a good laugh.

I saw my steady progress, as well as good and terrible decisions I had made, because I had captured my personal history to review from time to time. I began to understand my life's purpose, when and where my healing began, as I nurtured myself through writing. I also realized that when I didn't write, my life occasionally spun out of control.

Learning things about yourself teaches you who you are. It's a documentary of thoughts. Today many of us give credence to other people's proclamations about us, but it's time to explore and get to know ourselves. I love myself, so I can love you without a second thought. It was important for me to discover love and forgiveness, and it improved my outlook on life and my thoughts about others. I've consistently journaled since 1988, and my journal has been a spring of words revealing infinite possibilities. I see my mother's talents resonating in me, and I embrace every one of them, for she was a great woman with much insight. When I read through my journals, I realize how every word represents a pivotal moment to privately correct and teach myself, thus transforming into a new and better me. Journaling is a journey of hidden secrets that transform into open realities if you choose to make it happen. I would suggest that every young girl write her thoughts in a journal, and ideally others will respect her privacy and allow her to privately create her future thoughts and expressions.

Journaling is an intimate passage of thoughts, ideas, hurts, pains, pleasures, and discoveries. It gives you tools to know yourself and document your discoveries along the way through words, symbols, and your relationship with yourself. Love yourself enough to write declarations that support your goals and vision. Music is also an intricate part of the journey, for the right music can transform your moods and temperament. I listen to all genres, and I'm inspired by my favorite jazz musicians: Kirk Whalum, Ronnie Laws, George Howard, and Donald Byrd, to name just a few. You can have a great relationship with your parents, family, friends, pastor, and God—but you must have a relationship with yourself and get to know yourself.

Journaling is the passageway to self-discovery.

JOURNAL

I AM

 PAGE 2

What words would you use to describe yourself?

 PAGE 3

What favorite quotations encourages you?

 PAGE 4

A place for your thoughts ... Spill the tea!

 PAGE 4

Be joyful always. You are one of God's best creations. May God's kindness and love always be with you.

Glenda K. Rose

Love yourself.

 I am beautiful. I am blessed.

FAVORITE QUOTATIONS

 I AM INSPIRED. I AM ENCOURAGED. I BELIEVE IN
MYSELF. I AM FREE.

MY THOUGHTS

THE DIVA FILES

A Cultivated Woman

When a woman yields herself to God, she becomes wiser because her intellect is ruled by divine intelligence and knowledge. What does this mean? She surrenders her intellect for a greater intelligence called Spirit Life. The Holy Spirit becomes the motivating companion who helps her craft and develop the supernatural power that resides within her. A cultivated woman is groomed from the inside out. She is a guiding light, an act of pure love for others to see and follow. A spirit-filled woman cultivates mentors and enlightens generations.

A Woman of Virtue

A woman of virtue possesses faith, hope, charity, fortitude, justice, prudence, and temperance. Find the definitions of each virtue and write about your thoughts on them. You might possess one or two of these virtues already. However, we are builders, and to reach our highest good, we must continue climbing the ladder of character to assist humanity. The more virtuous women we create, the better our society will become.

Spirit Life

A woman must prepare herself for a spiritual journey. Learning and knowing who she is and why she was born is vital, but this truth can be revealed only by the Holy Spirit. Set aside time every day to seek what God sees in you, knowing that ultimately it will be greater than what you imagined for yourself. God has awesome plans for you, and spending time seeking a spiritual life will be time well spent.

Purpose

There's a lot of talk about purpose, but only God can download that information into your spirit. Everyone was born at a special time for a specific reason. I always wondered why some babies are born in the morning rather than the evening, why some babies come to earth before or after their delivery date, and so on. The logical reason for early or late births is incorrect calculation of the conception date, but I believe it's much more than that. Everyone will have to explore their own reasons. It is your job to explore all possibilities and opportunities. Don't be afraid to ask questions that point the way to a purposeful life. Most importantly, the all-knowing inner voice will speak to you. Take time to "Be still and know that I am God" (Psalm 46:10 NIV).

Vision

We are given vision so that we can practice seeing as far as possible, and create and develop thought in our everyday reality. When we develop, we build gardens within our souls, here on earth as in heaven. Envision heaven within you and create it here on earth, so the kingdom of God may be seen through you. Use your imagination to create heaven on earth.

Create

To imagine is to expect and conceive using one's inner ability to create, just like God did. God had a concept in mind, and he took six days to deliver creativity and manifest his thoughts. On the sixth day, he created the animals, then he made men and women in his own image, and on the seventh day he rested. Look at how powerful this can be! If we spend time building a relationship with the Holy Spirit, we can create anything in six days and rest on the seventh day, or in six months and rest in the seventh month, or in six years and rest in the seventh year. Here lies a basic strategy to help us implement creative plans. The days of the week should be used to balance your workload. On the seventh day, rest and declare that it is finished!

Hold Your Position

Whatever God has given you to do, whatever resonates as truth for you, hold that thought and stand in your rightful place. Sometimes we jump ship because of uncertainties, insecurities, and other people's opinions. When the appointed time arrives, we are missing in action because we moved from our designated assignment. We checked out of the appointed geographic location and missed the very opportunity for which we had been waiting. I don't think any of us do this intentionally, but it happens often. The Bible tells us to hold steadfast, "Be still and know that I am God," and keep the faith, because joy comes in the morning. All these brilliant little messages are to keep us anchored, watchful, and still.

A longtime acquaintance taught me to hold my position, and she was so right. Now I'm passing it on to you. What is your position, and how do you hold it? Your position is your slot in life. If it's your desire to run for class president, hold that thought in faith until you become president, and do not back down or move away from your desire. Hold on to your dreams and your assignment, and don't let anyone talk you out of it or into something different. When the appointed time comes, you will have positioned yourself in the right place and the appropriate time.

The Voice

You are a voice for your generation, so use it to empower, evoke, proclaim, declare, and transform. Use your voice as a loud trumpet; it is your communicator between earth and the supernatural. When you speak your position and move in your purpose, the right audience will hear you, and heaven will back you when you use your voice properly. The television show called *The Voice* is a good example of how that works in heaven. When you sing the right notes and speak the right words, it gets the attention of the judge, who will respond.

Praise

It is said that we should give thanks, and rightfully so. First Thessalonians 5:18 (NIV) tells us to always give thanks in everything. Praise God for who he is and for choosing you for the task at hand. Praise him through music, words, and silent thoughts, and praise him to others. He will inhabit your praises, which will help you gain access to his courts—and eventually his presence—to receive divine knowledge and wisdom. Praise is the key that unlocks doors.

Forgiveness

There is no simpler way to be forgiven than to forgive. You must give forgiveness in order to receive it.

Gifts of the Spirit

Wisdom, understanding, counsel, might, knowledge, and fear of the Lord: these characteristics govern the circles of beauty. Ask for them, and you will receive these marvelous gifts. Practice them, and you will shine. When you wear these gifts, they become a fixture on your spiritual wall, and you become a spiritual gift to all of humankind.

Freedom

Never abuse your freedom or anyone else's. Understand that true freedom comes from the one who set you free in the first place. Respect other people's points of view, and allow them to be themselves. This allows you to remain free in spirit, mind, body, and soul. The moment you control, you will be controlled or influenced by otherness, a force outside of universal law, and the principles of God will be violated. You have freedom and the right to choose—the power to act, speak, or think as you desire—without hindrance or restraint. You must allow others to practice that same freedom within the boundaries of universal law. We reap what we sow—or if you call it *karma*, you will get the same results—so use your freedom wisely (see John 8:36 NIV).

Laughter

I love to be humorous. Make sure you have people around you who can make you laugh. Laughter is good for the soul. In the Circle of Beauty, balance is necessary. Laughter balances and stabilizes our thoughts and emotions; it is the design for peaceful harmony. Proverbs 17:22 (NIV) says, "A merry heart doeth good like a medicine: but a broken spirit driest the bones." A merry heart improves the body and a depressed spirit dries the bones. Live and laugh out loud.

Balance

Recognize when you are out of balance and take the time to get back into divine alignment through prayer and self-evaluation. A false balance is an abomination to the Lord, and a just weight is his delight.

Circles of Beauty

The Circle of Beauty is a circle of values, ethics, integrity, and love.

Once we recognize the fact that every individual is a treasure of hidden and unsuspected qualities, our lives become richer, our judgement and our world is righter. It is not love that is blind; it is only the unnoticed eye that cannot see the real qualities of people.
—Charles H. Percy

GLAMOR

Godly Living Attracts Men
of Righteousness

GODLY

What does it mean to be godly? Some people think that being a godly woman is boring but it is anything *but* boring. In fact, it should be one of the highest offices on earth. Godly women are the very nature and character of God evolving into his love and power. Let's first look at women from the beginning of time. Genesis 1:27 (NIV) says, "Let us make man in our own image. In God's image he created him; male and female he created him." We were created in the image and likeness of our Supreme Father, creator of the universe. The plan for you and me was in the mind of God, the grandeur of his beauty and feminine presence.

God created man for woman and woman for man, and he formed woman last. "So, the last will be first, and the first will be last" (Matthew 20:16 NIV). I believe creating us last has made us first. Today women are moving forward and taking our rightful places with or without a fight, for we are determined to reign within our God-given status. I further believe that women are powerful weapons and can be weapons of mass destruction, though ideally we will use our power only for good. Proverbs 8:22 (NIV) mentions how wisdom was created by God and was present as a feminine presence during creation. There have been many explanations of this, but I will let you draw your own wise conclusions. I found it quite interesting that she—wisdom—accompanied God during his mighty act of creation.

I smile to myself and think about the potential that women have to shape our world into something extraordinary. Women's movements are evolving around the world, some more visibly than others, but they're all doing remarkable things to bring about social transformation. I commend you to keep serving and attracting good toward others, for the fruit of your work will become evident through the lives you touch.

Of course, we still have some blinders that must be removed. First, some of us, including sisters of all races, have forsaken our divinity as goddesses and now are recognized as bitches rather than as the queens we were created to be. The media has happily watched women fight, curse, and twerk. To my sisters in the body of Christ, some of your actions in other areas, too, must be dealt with. I want to address my sisters with respect and humility, because how we treat one another in the body of Christ must be addressed. I have spoken with many women from all walks of life, and they have experienced a considerable amount of rejection and disrespect from the women in the temple. How can we can walk past one another and not greet each other with a holy kiss as commanded? (See 1 Thessalonians 5:26 NIV.) A holy kiss is a proper salutation, for it exemplifies endearment, love, and acceptance. To be a light to the world, we must first be the radiant light of God. "For it is not my enemy who insults me then I could endure; it is not a foe who rises against me from him I could hide, but it is you a woman like myself, my sister in Christ, my close friend. We shared sweet fellowship together, we walked with the crowd into the house of God" (1 Thessalonians 5:26 NIV).

How many times have we gossiped and spread malicious rumors about one another, in a sacred space where we once fellowshipped and broke bread together? Should we not lead by example? Love and unity should be felt when we attend any true church on any day of the week. This is for all women. These childish insecurities and competition have caused us to lose ourselves and our identities, and forget the simple practice of equality with one another, yet we demand it on our jobs and in organizations. Jealousy is tiring and has caused the best relationships to falter. We could be a dynamic team if we allowed collaboration and connection to do what they automatically do, which is to set and implement goals. Collaboration requires leadership skills; someone must lead while others follow. If we would just face one another with pure intentions, talk through our differences, and look for resolution, we would have better relationships and partnerships. Let's make a conscious effort to move past petty differences and cat fights, and to move past men who are dishonest and cheaters—which is usually the cause of our differences.

Some men are professional cheaters. You need to know what you're dealing with and decide whether you want to love it or leave it. Stop blaming one another. There are definitely women who don't care whether a man is in a relationship, but they're not the only ones to blame. Jesus stooped down and wrote in the dust with his finger, to let the one who has never sinned throw the first stone (John 8:1–11 NIV). See, ladies, this woman was left alone to suffer public scorn and shame. God demonstrated his love when he saw that she stood alone to be scrutinized by Pharisees and accusers. Where was the man, and why was he never addressed?

I've seen shows where women—some even with grown children—were taking off their earrings to fight other women over a man whom they had caught cheating. Is this our only solution, to violently confront one another while our daughters take mental notes? How about teaching them to walk away and value themselves first. You may want to speak with Ms. Jada Pinkett Smith and ask for a seat at the table. Have an *open discussion*. Finally, if you catch your man cheating, address him—not the other woman. Years ago, when women weren't so violent, they talked to the side chick, who would expose details about the cheater. (Today we call them receipts.) Now, I'm not letting the side chick off the hook, but let's go back to character, integrity, and morals. Fighting her is not going to change her morals, but it will diminish yours.

Today I can write this in my book because I can successfully say that sometimes you must move on. It's not easy when you have someone unworthy of trust, but in my case it helped me make a sound decision. I chose peace of mind, dignity, and self-worth, rather than name calling and a lost cause. A man or woman who has decided in his or her heart to cheat is going to cheat anyway. Your duty is to keep womanhood in the kingdom recognizable as royal queens and elect ladies. The queen of England isn't the only queen, yet women will stand outside her palace for hours to gaze at her. There's nothing wrong with that, but look in the mirror. You forgot who you were called to be.

Godliness is the woman who maintains her divinity and her godly character, as she is commissioned by God to usher in his virtues to humankind. You, my lady, are the universal womb, the birthing canal for the entire world. From you, everything is produced. You are the sacred Garden of Eden, the soil of the earth. In you lies the fruit of good and evil, so you must choose to operate on a higher level of consciousness. How you act and carry yourself indicates whether you're the bitch or Divine Woman. Matthew 7:15–20 (NIV) says, "You will know them by their fruits." What fruit are you producing?

No longer can you say there aren't any good men. You attract what you are. If you consider yourself to be a sex symbol with your bosoms hanging out, you will attract the same—men who are only looking for sex and drama. They're looking for a good time, not for a wife or a godly woman. Instead of companionship, they're looking for a mammy, someone's breast the baby boy can lay his head on. I get tired of just talking about it; we need to wake up. We are God's gatekeepers in society, preserving our queenship throughout generations. We must change perceptions by producing godly characteristics.

I, wisdom, dwell with prudence,
And find out knowledge and discretion.
The fear of the Lord is to hate evil;
Pride and arrogance and the evil way
And the perverse mouth I hate.
Counsel is mine, and sound wisdom;
I am understanding, I have strength.
By me kings reign,
And rulers decree justice.
By me princes' rule, and nobles,
All the judges of the earth.
I love those who love me,
And those who seek me diligently will find me.
Riches and honor are with me,
Enduring riches and righteousness.
My fruit is better than gold, yes, than fine gold,
And my revenue than choice silver.
I traverse the way of righteousness,
In the midst of the paths of justice,
That I may cause those who love me to inherit wealth,
That I may fill their treasuries.
The Lord possessed me at the beginning of His way,
Before His works of old.
I have been established from everlasting,
From the beginning, before there was ever an earth.
When there were no depths I was brought forth,
When there were no fountains abounding with water.
Before the mountains were settled,
Before the hills, I was brought forth;
While yet He had not made the earth or the fields,
Or the primal dust of the world.
When He prepared the heavens, I was there,
When He drew a circle on the face of the deep,
When He established the clouds above,
When He strengthened the fountains of the deep,
When He assigned to the sea its limit,

So that the waters would not transgress His command,
When He marked out the foundations of the earth,
Then I was beside Him as a master craftsman;
And I was daily His delight,
Rejoicing always before Him,
Rejoicing in His inhabited world,
And my delight was with the sons of men.
Now therefore, listen to me, my children,
For blessed are those who keep my ways.
Hear instruction and be wise,
And do not disdain it.
Blessed is the man who listens to me,
Watching daily at my gates,
Waiting at the posts of my doors.
For whoever finds me finds life,
And obtains favor from the Lord;
But he who sins against me wrongs his own soul;
All those who hate me love death.

—Proverbs 8:12–36 (NKJV)

Circles of Beauty is an invisible beauty that serves,
acknowledges, and creates beauty in everything it touches.

LIVING

How are you living? The quality of your life is important to God: "Beloved: I pray that in all things that you may prosper in every way and that your body may keep well, even as I know your soul keeps" (3 John 1:2 NIV). You should live a high-quality life in all aspects of your being, for we were created to live well. Your lifestyle reflects your creator, and his splendor should shine through you. While you were growing up, your parents did not allow you out of the house looking shabby. They understood that you represented the family name, so they made sure you maintained a polished look.

Ladies, do you realize that your child's behavior is your responsibility? I know what you're thinking—*What about the father?* —but let's look at what Proverbs says about training our children. A child left unattended brings shame to the mother (Proverbs 29:15 NIV). The Bible is clear that the mother has the responsibility of training her children in ethics and manners. This doesn't mean that if a child goes a little wayward, the mother did not do her job. But it's a quick reminder that if we don't properly care for our children, society will blame the mother. Isn't it the mother who stands before society when there are difficult matters against her children and the mother who has endless hope for her seed even when society differs? The mother shapes the family's image, manners, positive speech, etiquette, and style, and her duties continually evolve as she shapes her part of society—her family.

How we live in our environment will produce fruit. Have you ever smelled fruit after it went bad and immediately you wanted to get rid of the odor? It's the same way in society, bad fruit produces a stench of crime, disorderly conduct, and rebellion, and the list goes on. It would serve all of us well to recognize that our fruit will one day be a contributor to society, and the things they have learned will affect us all, so ideally it will be productive.

We are to live our best lives, whatever that entails. We must find our niches and create the best lives possible for ourselves and our families. My Aunt Francine, rest her soul, lived in an urban environment, and many things took place outside her residence. But when you walked into her home, the atmosphere was surprisingly different from what you'd expect. She built a beautiful indoor playhouse in the basement for my siblings and me, and her backyard was filled with beautiful flowers and a vegetable garden. She made small spaces into oases. The outward environment did not affect the beauty that resonated inside her. She created an atmosphere for queens and kings, no matter what was going on around her. This fine woman was known for having the most beautiful home on her block. My Aunt Francine prepared the best meals, and she made time for our spiritual studies by taking us to mass or reading Bible stories to us. Unlike today, when she walked down the street, everyone stopped what they were doing to salute her, and she was well respected in her community.

Like many others, my auntie was a great mentor and teacher. She taught us that where we lived did not have to cripple us and that what we did with what we had was the key to obtaining more. Her portrait of life was identical to my mother's. Those two beautiful souls knew the secret to beauty, that the inner person compels you to become a beautiful woman on the outside. Life is what you make of it. You can have a pleasant life even if you don't have everything you think you need; just use your imagination to create it. I love the movie *Hook*, which I watched repeatedly with my children when they were younger. In one scene, there was no food on the table, and they all cheered Peter on, saying, "Imagine it, Peter. Use your imagination." Peter Pan forgot who he really was on the inside. Full of power and creativity, he had to reactivate his imagination to create food for his hungry disciples.

Your faith is your imagination. You are commanded by God in all things to prosper. Whatever you imagine or desire can be yours; the possibility already exists in the heavens. When Peter saw the dark picnic, the table was bare, but he imagined it full of delightful dishes—and eventually he spoke that into existence. Even Peter Pan realized there is no lack in the universe, so he created a feast rather than a famine. Do you who have seen the movie remember all the lavish food Peter created for the rest of his disciple friends who chose to assist him throughout his journey?

You have allowed the illusion of scarcity to play out in your mind for so long that you have created the special effect of poverty. If you practice what Peter did, your voice will be heard in the heavens, and the angels will begin to implement your commands. It's ironic that Peter Pan's first name is Peter, just like Peter in the Bible; both had followers and the power to make things come alive!

In the Circle of Beauty, you have a voice. How you use it will determine how you live! Ask yourself this question now: *How am I living?*

Faith is your imagination.

Life is either a daring adventure or nothing.
—Helen Keller

Live
Laugh
Love

ATTRACT

Okay, we've all heard that you attract what you are. With ladies, your thoughts and imaginations lure different experiences and relationships into your lives. What are you hoping for? What are your desires? What do you want to attract into your life that's different from what you are getting now? After answering these questions, start working toward what you want. Move toward the thing you're seeking. In most cases, there should be similar characteristics and attributes to attract the type of people you want in your inner circle. If you do not move toward what you're seeking, you'll probably not experience it. For example, if you desire to work or date someone in theater, you must go in that direction, perhaps by taking an acting class or visiting theater venues. I know they say opposites attract, but I've always questioned that. Are they really opposites, or could the other person reflect your own hidden potential?

Women tend to push relationships to the next level even when they should remain platonic. A woman who is lonely and desires companionship probably will move based on emotion and need. Through the years, I've had good male friends. Bernard and I met in college when I was seventeen years old, and our relationship has remained platonic for forty-four years with lots of fun and laughter. Some friendships can turn into strong marriages, but do not push—just let everything flow naturally. We should learn from our mistakes. You know the old saying "Insanity is when you keep doing the same thing over and over again, expecting different results." Does this sound familiar? Were the last two or three guys you dated all cheaters—different ages, living in different cities, but running the same game? Is this because there are no good men, or is there a cheater in you? Just asking … Again, explore why you keep repeating the same scenario.

Could it be the nature of the men you choose? I have an acquaintance whose papa was a rolling stone, and please believe me—so is he. It's in his DNA, and nobody's going to change that, but he has—with much prayer, strength, and counsel.

Prayer can change things, especially when accompanied by truth, strategy, focus, and purpose. I had a group of women praying for their mates, and I heard the voice of the Holy Spirit quietly say they were praying for things they weren't qualified to have. I was just as shocked as the women, whom I told. You cannot pray for a kingly guy unless you are a queenly woman, metaphorically speaking. You cannot pray for a wealthy man while you fail to pay your bills and credit cards. It is unlawful to ask for a big house with a luxury car when you do not maintain or treasure your current residence or vehicle. Some of you don't cook or clean, but your Instagram pictures look fabulous. Are you beginning to get the picture? You cannot request outside your realm of preparation and readiness. Have you ever heard Jesus's well-known parable of the ten virgins, also known as the parable of the wise and foolish virgins? According to Matthew 25:1–13 (NIV), the five virgins who prepared for the bridegroom's arrival were rewarded, whereas the five who weren't ready were disowned.

The Bible makes it clear that those who were prepared for the event were rewarded, but those who didn't prepare were ignored. Hmm … Are your prayers for a mate being ignored? I'm just asking so that you will put more thought into preparation as opposed to results. Are you willing to go the whole nine yards to get what you are praying for? Preparation is key; you must be willing to take on some of the challenges that will surface. From those to whom much is given, much is required. The game of life has a few basic principles, such as that some play better than others. The wise virgins played to win.

Pretty Woman and Cinderella stories don't happen in real life. I read a book about Jackie Kennedy years ago. She and her mother were focused players of the game of life. Jackie prepared herself to become the president's wife; she was well groomed, well spoken, educated, and confident. She insisted on learning French by studying in France rather than at Princeton, a decision that paid off after her husband became the president. The president of France was impressed that she spoke French fluently, resulting in a good relationship with JFK and phenomenal rewards. Jackie was introduced to the famous designer Valentino; while she was in France, he quickly became her designer, and she became iconic for her style and fashion savvy.

Preparation opens doors of opportunity. Most often, the people you meet will be in the sphere of influence with which you are familiar, and there are people in your future who have yet to appear. As you feed your mind with new knowledge, that will position you for the experiences you have imagined. You must allow yourself to be groomed for where you are headed. No fairy tales, since they are only imagined, but fairy tales can help if you search for the hidden treasure in the story.

As told in the Bible, the story of Esther is not a fairy tale. She was an orphan raised by her uncle Mordecai, whose job at the palace made it possible for Esther to go there often. Esther was chosen as a potential bride for the king, but not without grooming for the position. Other girls were selected to become potential queens, but they did not make the final cut. In the movie *One Night with the King*, all the girls who were waiting to have their one night with the king were allowed to indulge themselves in a room filled with jewels. The girls took more jewelry than they could possibly wear, and their bodies tipped over because of the weight of the jewels. Esther stayed behind as the other girls took excessive treasure. Not everything that glitters is the jackpot. Esther was wise enough to prepare for her meeting with the king by asking his servant what the king would like in the way of jewelry. He showed Esther a simple necklace, she wore it to see the king, and it turned out that he was a simple man who just wanted to be loved.

There are several principles in operation here:

1. Ask for nothing and possess it all.
2. Above all, get understanding (Proverbs 4:7 NIV). Wisdom is the principal thing.
3. Communicate, ask, and it shall be given (Matthew 7:7 NIV).

Esther got the right answers and proceeded to meet the king with knowledge, understanding, and favor from on high. Through preparation, she became queen and owned half of the king's inheritance, and the lives of many people were changed as a result.

I went into detail to explain that preparation affords power and advantage; no magic is involved. The right man does not just show up—you must prepare for him. I encourage you to write your vision and be specific. Make it plain, so that you will be able to read it and run with the vision. It's time to get moving!

Prepare

JOURNAL

PAGE 1

Circles of Beauty is an invisible beauty that serves, acknowledges, and creates beauty in everything it touches.

Success is where preparation and opportunity meet.

Proper preparation prevents poor performance.

A man who doesn't plan plans to fail.

I am preparing for …

MY THOUGHTS

MEN

I can give you my definition of a man, but that's just one perspective filled with opinions, past experiences, television, and movies. Okay, so how do we identify what kind of man we are dealing with—or should deal with? Better yet, what type of men do you want, as opposed to who you are currently attracting?

Let's go back to what the Bible says about a man. At least we can gain clarity on the subject through the book of life. "But if anyone does not provide for his relatives, and especially for members of his household, he has denied the faith and is worse than an unbeliever" (1 Timothy 5:8 ESV). The Bible makes it clear that a godly man must provide for his family. If the man you are considering dating has children, does he provide for them adequately? If he has elderly parents, does he help take care of them? You should observe his actions, which will demonstrate his character and how he handles his financial obligations. Is he a doer of the word of God? You do not want someone who attends church only and does not follow godly principles, which amounts to spiritual education with no transformation. I am sure you already know that this is an indication of how he will treat you. Righteous men understand what is required of them and follow through.

"For even when we were with you, we were given this command: If anyone is not willing to work, let him not eat" (2 Thessalonians 3:10 NIV). What is his work ethic like? Does the gentleman you are considering work? Does he offer to purchase groceries for you? Is he a giver or a taker? Is he generous with his time, or is his cell phone turned off when you try to call him? Is he missing in action on holidays? If he misses your birthday but expects you to celebrate his, you should probably run before he cripples your finances, time, and self-worth.

"I desire then that in every place the men should pray, lifting holy hands without anger or quarreling" (1 Timothy 2:8 ESV). What does he believe, and in whom does he believe? Is he easily angered, or is he understanding, with a considerable amount of patience? Have you bothered to find out if your spiritual beliefs will be compromised because of his unbelief? Is he a man who can pray for you and have faith in times of trouble? He must manage his own household well, with all dignity keeping his children submissive (1 Timothy 3:4 NIV). Today men leave their homes broken to pursue other relationships; he should make sure he leaves things in order without accusation and public shame.

Does he have a home, or is he always at your residence? How well does he manage his affairs, and with whom does he live? Have you been to his residence, or do you always meet in public places or at your cozy abode? How many children and baby mommas are in the circle, and how much child support does he pay? Is it enough to sustain two households? Make sure he is not just a sperm donor. These are things you should ask along the way, before it gets too serious. If he is evasive about basic questions, that may be a sign that an untold truth is lurking somewhere. Is he trustworthy, someone you could spend the rest of your life with? One thing I dislike is when a man blames his baby's momma for all his financial woes and shortcomings. This question is very important: does he take responsibility? If you are serious about him, you need to observe and stay awake, because there is a lot to consider before you get too serious. By the way, ladies, let's stop attacking one another. If there is a baby momma and you are planning on marrying him, have the conversation. Ask his ex-girlfriend questions, and work on blending the family with respect and honoring each other as women and mothers.

You should be mindful of his lifestyle, which is going to affect you and your financial portfolio. If you combine finances, and his life or yours is a financial wreck, your finances will go haywire sooner rather than later. An acquaintance of mine, who had just bounced back from a bad relationship, started a new job, moved into a new apartment, and purchased a new car. She attracted the same type of guy with the same kind of abuse, but she did not recognize it until after he moved in with her. She lost everything she had worked so hard for. Let's be wise in our decision-making. We have all experienced at least one relationship that was not what we expected. Perhaps we failed to ask the right questions and observe with hawk eyes. These days there is a lot of deception, whether it's self-deception or someone else's. Pay attention, because the clues are there.

There are good men out there. If you have not attracted one yet, that could mean he has not appeared on your radar just yet. Perhaps you need to make some simple social changes in your day-to-day life, rearrange your priorities, or rid yourself of some bad rubbish. I have found that when women don't dwell on not dating, someone worth their time will appear. Please don't think that every man is going to become your husband. Some women can't get past one date before marriage pops up in their minds. Enjoy dating the gentleman you're with, without unrealistic expectations. Thoughts—yours and his—can become a problem, so have a sensible conversation and be patient.

Yes, be selective, but not picky. You might have to date outside your culture. You might have to date the nerd instead of the pretty boy or the cool guy with swag who has a woman in every state. Choose character over looks. Think long and hard about your choices when it comes to dating or marrying a man. Marriage is a lifetime investment for the two of you. When you know for sure what you desire, you will raise new standards and ethical values, the keys to good decision-making. The silent voice of rightful thinking and choices lies within you. The lights that go off are warning signals, so pay close attention or you might get duped.

You be the glamor girl. (Godly living attracts men of righteousness.) Attract what you are. Don't go looking for him. Change your approach by preparing to meet someone but letting him find you. Presenting yourself means preparation, so go out and enjoy yourself without the fishing rod. The right man will approach you, or you will be introduced by someone in your circle of friends. All the possibilities are there. You must set yourself up to be seen without negative cues.

Your biological clock is in God's hands. When Harriet Tubman completed her assignment, a twenty-five-year-old man knocked on her door and proposed to her. She said yes, God restored her youthfulness, and they married. Harriet proved that time has nothing to do with finding the right man. Know your purpose first, and everything connected to your purpose will show up.

Be encouraged, never behave as a desperate or fearful woman. While single, enjoy high-quality time with friends and family, live out loud, experiment, travel, explore, grow, and qualify everything around you. Focus on those things that produce positive outcomes. Pray, prepare, and believe. There are good men, some better than others, but they're waiting to be discovered just as you are waiting to be found.

I, with a deeper instinct, choose a man who compels
my strength, who makes enormous demands on me,
who does not doubt my courage or my toughness,
who does not believe me naïve or innocent, who
has the courage to treat me like a woman.
—Anaïs Nin

Fly forward
and
do not
look back

RIGHTEOUSNESS: RECLAIMING OUR VIRTUE

First, we must understand what *virtue* really means. I used to think Mary, the mother of Jesus, or angels were the only symbols of virtue. I just did not believe virtue was attainable when I was younger. I thought there was some super-spiritual experience a person had to have to be considered virtuous. Several women in the Bible have virtuous characteristics, such as the woman in Proverbs 31 (NIV) who is described as virtuous or a woman of noble character. When you read all that she accomplished, she is a tough act to follow—or so I thought. Every Mother's Day, ministers would preach about this famous lady in the Bible, and oh, how I wanted to meet and chat with her, even though she was making all of us look bad. I wondered, what were her secrets for successful living?

Years ago, I had no idea how to duplicate her outstanding abilities in my own life. I just knew she had it going on and no one could live up to her extraordinary virtue. That woman was a manufacturer, importer, manager, real estate agent, farmer, fashion and interior designer, merchant, wife, and mother with servants who adored her. She was well known and her husband was well respected because of her. The Bible considers her virtuous, and I was sure there would never be another. Even the Bible asks, who can find another like her? Here's where it gets sticky. I believe the Bible means that women must look at her characteristics and find the hidden abilities within us that create a virtuous woman. The Bible doesn't mention that she went to church or prayed all day, but she did fear God and she was not an idle woman. The virtuous woman was an outstanding leader, an entrepreneur with integrity; she wasn't considered virtuous simply because she was religious.

I saw the movie *How Stella Got Her Groove Back* several times with girlfriends. Later that year I dreamed that I was staying at an economy hotel in Jamaica. When I asked the bellboy if he could tell me where Stella stayed, he pointed to a beautiful hotel across the street, and off I went to the posh, glass-encased hotel. When I walked into the lobby and put my luggage down, the Spirit of God spoke to me: "Tell the women of God to go get their groove back." Don't kill the messenger just yet! Stella had her issues, but she also had virtuous characteristics. She knew how to have fun, thanks to her friend. Stella was a businesswoman on Wall Street who eventually quit her job to become an entrepreneur/author, and then her book and movie made her millions. Just like the virtuous woman in the Bible, she set about her work vigorously and made it happen. Stella cared for her son, as well as other family members from time to time, giving them the best of the best.

The virtuous woman cared for her family and servants as well. Proverbs 31:27 (NIV) tells us that she watched over the affairs of her household, and Proverbs 31:11 (NIV) says, "Her husband has full confidence in her and lacks nothing of value." Stella's husband encouraged her to pursue what she really loved by crafting a studio for her to work in, and he supported her decision to lay aside her career and pursue her passion. I know, I know—they later divorced. But he jump-started the vision and pointed her toward her true destiny to become a wealthy and famous writer, so perhaps that was his soul purpose. May I propose to you that Stella had some of the same virtuous characteristics as the woman mentioned in Proverbs?

Let's look at another biblical figure whom God considered righteous. Rahab, the prostitute, was considered righteous for lodging spies in her home (James 2:25 NIV). She too had a business and was able to quickly negotiate a deal to save herself and her family from the judgment of the God of Israel. Biblical interpreters have acknowledged Rahab as a woman of hospitality, mercy, faith, and patience. Rahab became a paragon of virtue and married into a prominent family, of Salmon from the tribe of Judah, the father of Boaz, who is mentioned in the genealogy of Christ.

I further propose to the women in the house of God that you go get your groove back and reclaim your virtue. Start the business you've always dreamed about, earn your real estate license, open that boutique and start a clothing line or fashion house. If you enjoy gardening, start a nursery business or a community garden, or contract with the public schools to teach a horticultural class. You need Stella and Stella needs you! She can help you jump-start your business goals, and you can help her with her spiritual walk. Don't throw the baby out with the bathwater. Just because Stella does not fit into a religious category doesn't mean she cannot possess God-given characteristics of virtue. News flash! You don't possesses all of them either!

We are all works in progress, some of us more than others. Jesus was in the business of saving lives, and he owns all the gold and silver and the cattle on a thousand hills. These women have exemplified Christlike characteristics that we all need to build a kingdom. Virtue is a lifestyle for the total and complete woman, and her virtue is manifested in various forms and stages in life. Let's refine our thinking and be all that we desire. Who can find a virtuous woman? We all have virtues to contribute to society, just like the woman in Proverbs 31 (NIV).

From now on, when we look at one another, let's see what God sees in us. Then maybe our virtue will be more noticeable than our sin. It's time for a change. We must stop making people feel like outcasts because they have not come into the kingdom according to our personal standards. If we show more love and respect for one another, everyone's virtue will be identifiable. My motto is "It takes one to know one." I believe we can help transform the world into a place of unity and value. We need to be more inviting, so that other people will desire to know more about the things of God and his glory. We need to do more to empower the kingdom through economics and community growth. Girl, go get your groove back and do it with style and character. Be the unstoppable virtuous woman.

Virtue consists of you producing, creating, and forming. Mary and Elizabeth, those biblical women, had it going on. They had no identity crises whatsoever, because they were united through purpose and vision. We must step up our game and become biblical leaders of success. No longer can we afford to *talk* God—we must *become* God in the playing field of life. It's time to represent God by building high-quality relationships and businesses across nations. Learn how to live on purpose—what a cliché, but it's true. I have met many women who are not stepping up to their place of potential. Some are still waiting and trusting God for what he has already qualified them to have. I commend the women who have done that, and I urge other women to do so right now. We play a major role in job creation, and when there are more jobs, the economy thrives, and people are a lot happier. We need more women entrepreneurs as role models, connecting like-minded women to explore and reclaim their virtuous gifts.

I finally can relate to the Proverbs 31 (NIV) woman. She's not just a biblical figure to discuss, but a public figure who demonstrated excellent leadership skills. Her life story provides the checks and balances that we all need to move forward. In the Circle of Beauty, virtue is a woman handling her business with integrity and without prejudice and judgment.

BEAUTY, THE BEAST TAMER

I'm sure many of you saw the movie *Beauty and the Beast*. Do you remember how Belle tamed the beast into a charming prince? Let's be clear: All of us have a beast nature lurking inside that needs taming from time to time, for some more often than for others. Surprised? Don't be. The last time someone cut you off in traffic, did you give them the finger or call them an ass (or something even worse)? We've all had that experience, right? The beast emerges when we are angered or wounded. Nowadays young girls fight over boys and put the video on Facebook, grown women fight on reality shows and call each other provocative names, and children argue and fight with their parents. Depression is a beast, as we saw in the movie, and that beast stayed locked in one room. Unfortunately we see the beast frequently through various circumstances. What is the beast tamer? The fruits of the Spirit—love, joy, peace, long-suffering, kindness, goodness, faithfulness, gentleness, and self-control—orchestrated by our friend, the talented Holy Spirit.

In case you haven't met or even heard of the Holy Spirit, I will introduce him to you shortly. He was sent by God to tame the beast in us all. When we allow him access, the fruits of the Spirit give birth to good things in people. The Holy Spirit helps us have a more loving nature that will transform evil and wickedness into love and mercy. However, the Holy Spirit has a huge job on his hands compared with Belle, who had only one beast to transform. Belle tamed the beast by demonstrating love and patience, and she eventually marries the beast she tamed.

We all marry what we join ourselves to, whether it be man, woman, or principle. "Make a tree good and its fruit will be good, make a tree bad and its fruit will be bad; for a tree is known by its fruit" (Matthew 12:33

NIV). Belle was from a good tree; she had been taught to be loving and kind, and she loved and honored her father. Throughout the story, Belle and her father demonstrated love and respect for one another; an apple doesn't fall far from the tree. "Honor your father and your mother, so that you may live long in the land the Lord your God is giving you" (Exodus 20:12 NIV). Belle was married to the principle of love and kindness; no matter how frustrated she became, she finished her assignment. Even with all the distractions along the way, she finished the race and won the prize. Everything around her was transformed, right down to the dishes in the cabinet. The furniture rejoiced, the atmosphere shifted, and everything became beautiful in its own time (Ecclesiastes 3:11 NIV). Her mansion was filled with the fruits of the spirit and the splendor of joy.

Beauty reigns!

Beauty is eternity gazing at itself in a mirror,
But you are eternity and you are the mirror.
—Kahlil Gibran

MEET THE HOLY SPIRIT: JESUS GAVE US THE GREATEST GIFT

> The angel answered, "The Holy Spirit will come on you, and the power of the Most High will overshadow you. So, the holy one to be born will be called the Son of God."

> —Luke 1:35 (NIV)

The key word is *power*. The Holy Spirit is the power that permeates us to transform the human heart. When he overshadows us, we manifest the love of God, creating a new humanity. The Holy Spirit comes to transform selfishness and evil into love, so that the living word of God comes alive through us. Take a moment to ask God to come into your hearts. Romans 10:13 (NKJV) says, "For whoever calls on the name of the Lord shall be saved." The Holy Spirit helps us to forgive, because as women we can be harsh with ourselves and one another. The Holy Spirit saves us from our feelings of inadequacy. Some women are ashamed of their past failures, and families and a host of insecurities and fears can cripple us. But all these miserable feelings are gladly overshadowed by the Holy Spirit, who rescues us from negative thoughts that can destroy our future and gives us as many fresh starts as we need.

> To bestow on them a crown of Beauty instead of Ashes, the oil of joy instead of mourning and a garment of praise instead of a spirit of despair.

> —Isaiah 61:3 (NIV)

Inspiration originates with the Holy Spirit in man's spirit.
—Watchman Nee

SUCCESSFUL BEAUTY

When we succeed in various areas of our lives, within the Circle of Beauty, we reach out and touch raw beauty in others. Many times, we can see potential and possibilities in other people, but we sometimes fail to acknowledge, help, or inspire them to pursue their highest good. Helping someone succeed is part of your success. God does not forget, and the universe will reward you in special ways for acts of warmheartedness. Most often we are totally unaware of the rewards and blessings we have acquired through simple acts of thoughtfulness and kindness; it's easy to forget to count your blessings when you have so many.

You can never be successful without gratitude. Reaching out and sharing with people who are less fortunate is an act of God. Being less fortunate doesn't necessarily mean being poor; many people have never been loved or experienced true friendship or family. Isaiah 54:1 (NIV) says, "Sing, barren woman, you who never bore a child; burst into song, shout for joy, you who were never in labor; because more are the children of the desolate woman than of her who has a husband." For many years the Holy Spirit led me to that scripture. I did not think it pertained to me since I had three children and had previously been married. How wrong I was! Yes, I had children, but I had not birthed my dreams and aspirations, which left me in a state of desolation. How wonderful is it that God saw my barrenness and untouched potential and creativity? Not only did he see it, but he promised me that I would no longer be barren, and he assured me that I would become fruitfully creative.

If you have ever felt barren, rejoice! There is hope! Pick up the Bible and ask God to make Isaiah 54 (NIV) a reality in your life. In the Circle of Beauty, you are the beautiful hands of God, and he can reach out and touch someone's life through you. Beauty successfully circulates around the world. The path to beauty is enormous, but you must be able to see it before it blossoms. I don't have to like what you do or what you stand for, but I accept you as God's creative handiwork. I accept and acknowledge you as a human being. We all deserve to be loved, and I love you!

Capture beauty whenever possible—a child holding its father's hand, a dog rolling playfully on the grass. These are all beautiful moments to remember. At a park in Europe, I saw a young couple playing and rolling around on the grass. When I took a photo of the beautiful moment of glee, the couple saw me and began to laugh hysterically. I just laughed with them and took another picture. I was able to chime in and feel the joy of laughter, which is truly contagious. We can find beauty in the simplest things, and it radiates when we recognize its presence. God uses laughter to heal our pain. Don't allow your woes to drown out the simple pleasures that beauty adds to our lives.

I've watched the *Ellen DeGeneres Show* many times, and it has brought laughter and tears to my eyes as she shares the wealth of her success with others. Sometimes the stories are sad, and other times she just blesses people with gifts for the fun of it. I believe she and Oprah Winfrey set the stage for giving back to their audience, and how beautiful it has been to see others follow suit. It is incredible to watch and share in the joy of giving. If all of humankind just gave back, we would all be happier and wealthier. There really is no lack in the world; greed overshadows the gift of giving, and it is an evil act. There will always be people who will turn something beautiful into something ugly by taking advantage of others' generosity. However, the universe is the judge and the jury. Hold fast to integrity! You reap what you sow.

Not one drop of my self-worth depends
on your acceptance of me.
You cannot afford to be that vulnerable.

SELF-WORTH

Self-worth cannot be totally defined through events and experiences in a person's life. If you have had unpleasant experiences, do not allow that to deter you from being yourself. An unpleasant experience does not have to be permanent; it can simply be a snapshot to document your progress. So how does a person formulate self-esteem? I watched an interview with girls who had become strippers, and despite other people's opinions of them, they focused on their long-term goals and insisted they had not lost their sense of self-worth. Some of these young women were in college, and others were single mothers caring for their children and needed money to purchase a home. They all had reasons for choosing this part-time gig. I am not advocating stripping as a goal, but this story demonstrates that no matter what your past may have been, you do not have to allow it to cripple your self-esteem. Despite what others think about you, maintain positive feelings of self-worth and values that consistently line up with what God says about you. We are all valuable in his sight.

There are women in the Bible who had undesirable pasts, but Jesus covered them without condemnation. The young women whom I saw in the interview did not allow that moment in time to determine who they were or what they would become. One young woman eventually went to medical school, and another bought a home for her family and went back to school. I commend these women, who did not allow public opinion to dictate their futures. The goals they set for themselves were eventually accomplished. They all agreed that if they could do it all over, they would not choose that route, but at that time they did not see any other way. The interviewer could have tried to diminish their self-worth, but the interview was done with grace. The goal was to tell their stories—why and how women find themselves working as strippers. This documentary will help other young women choose wisely, and when mistakes are made, we can correct them and still deem ourselves worthy. If you have someone around whom you look up to, pay attention to what they do—or even go a step further and ask them to mentor you. Having a mentor shortens the distance to achieve your goals. Sharing your hopes and dreams with a mentor can help put things in perspective. A true mentor will not allow you to stay in the valley of sorrow and negative thoughts. They will inspire and motivate you to continue your journey until you conquer the giants in your life. You can create your own life however you choose. When you're young, there are many distractions that can deter you away from your purpose. Write down your vision no matter how long the list, you will eventually incorporate, delete, strategize, implement, and gain momentum.

Set lofty standards for yourself, but I caution you—setting noble standards does not make you better than other people. It just means you are making choices suitable for yourself. Superiority has no place in the Circle of Beauty. Every soul has value, although not every soul is yet aware of just how valuable they are; hopefully, in time, they will awaken to Gods majestic kingdom. My hope is that we will all take a second look at our worth and value, who we are, and the power we have been given to create a beautiful and successful soul with humility.

Humility is a badge of honor.

CLOSING

Circles of Beauty

In closing, remember who you are. You are wired for success and designed to be God's glory on earth. God dwells in each one of us in different ways. It is up to you to see God in all things and in all people and acknowledge the beauty of his presence.

The many faces of God are black and white, light and bright, heavy and small, big and tall, short and stout, intelligent and wise.

The Circle of Beauty is a creative well filled with treasure, some unheard, and too many to tell or measure.

Beauty gifts the world with bells, whistles, and words that restore, repair, and glisten. The powers of love refreshes the air, so pay attention and listen.

Acceptance is a beautiful delight. Honor is the joy of our soul. Unity is the glue that forges us together.

Peace is the stillness of quiet differences.

Beauty is the spirit of God that dwells in us all!

In a world where you can be anything, be yourself.
—author unknown

Circles of Beauty is a curriculum that can be taught in schools and various organizations, at speaking engagements, and through motivational seminars. Contact can be made through email at lovelyglendarose@gmail.com or by phone at (213) 292-3430.

Peace and beautiful grace,
Glenda K. Rose Freeman

ABOUT THE AUTHOR

Glenda K. Rose is a motivational writer, speaker, and coach. She lives in California and mentors girls and young women. Glenda has traveled throughout the United States and internationally with a message of empowerment: "The most successful woman is the woman who is not afraid to be herself." Her messages are practical, addressing many issues, such as esteeming one another as women and creating contagious atmospheres of love, kindness, honesty, truth, and self-worth. Self-love is a universal vibration that can be felt even in just passing one another. Love is a strong energy that transforms humankind, animals, and nature. We will never see true transformation until it radiates through us. We are the reflection of our creator, who is pure love with nothing missing or broken. Ms. Rose says it should be a women's priority to maintain her inner beauty. When she understands the value and treasure that is within, she will nurture her inward beauty first and love will do the rest.

Ms. Rose has a unique way of addressing and teaching social conduct and practices, and her seminars are innovative and encouraging. No matter where you live, love is a contagious universal action that can be understood on many levels. Glenda Rose charges the atmosphere with cohesiveness and a sense of belonging. Out of her own rejection, she has made it a priority to unify the women with whom she surrounds herself. If we are willing to adjust our attitudes and personalities to see through the eyes of our creator, we will see one another as ourselves.

Glenda majored in organizational communications and attended school for image consulting and visual arts. She loves to color the lives of other people through conferences, seminars, podcasts, and conference calls. Ms. Rose has three sons, whom she loves and treasures. Although she does not have daughters, every young girl she mentors becomes a part of the Circle of Beauty family.

Printed in the United States
By Bookmasters